Härte

More praise for *Härte*

Sade LaNay writes from the space between the vulnerability of strength and the strength of vulnerability. Confident, revealing, beautiful, and painful. ***Härte*** contains a subtle linguistic music and brutal confrontation. It's impossible to resist **LaNay**'s poetry.

—Aase Berg

A challenge for those addicted to monolingual work, **Sade LaNay**'s fascinating new collection, ***Härte***—German for hardness, cruelty—contains uncanny tercets composed between languages we mis/take and carry beyond linguistic convention. ***Härte*** is the soft wax become hard seal, the malleable word violated to make an impression, trauma spoken in the confabulation of a generative translation con/founded to forge prolific signification. Trans/duction, trance/formation: musical, mystical, and harsh verse to be chewed in the mouth and the mind.

—Lisa Rose Bradford

Härte

Sade LaNay

DOWNSTATE
LEGACIES
Normal, Illinois

DOWNSTATE
LEGACIES

Published by Downstate Legacies
Illinois State University
4241 Publications Unit
Normal, Illinois 61790-4241
http://english.illinoisstate.edu/pubunit/

Distributed to the trade by Small Press Distribution
1341 Seventh Street, Berkeley, CA 94710
www.spdbooks.org

Cover and Book Design: Publications Unit,
    Department of English, Illinois State University,
    Director: Steve Halle, Production Assistant:
    Jennifer Glasscock

ISBN: 978-0-9974041-3-5
First Edition

for SJ & Martha & Anna
thank you for the gentleness

Wathint' abafazi, wathint' imbokodo'
       –1956 Women's March in Pretoria, South Africa

Everything is goop. I long for that alchemical thing where the meaning was the sound—wherein the sound of the word can actually imitate experience.
                                          –Sarah Ruhl

Hardening does not eliminate what made hardening seem necessary: that sense of being too soft, too receptive; too willing to receive an impression. Hardness is a relative condition even when we try and relate differently to a condition. What we become to withstand can become something that hardens us from others, those who might be closest, who might too have to survive the weather. We can damage each other in how we survive being damaged.
                                          –Sara Ahmed

Finding Words for *Härte*

SITTING NEXT TO SADE ON MONDAY AFTERNOONS, as they were working on *Härte*, I temporarily became the flesh and blood extension of the German dictionary apps on our phones. I assumed that I knew German well. After all, I had spent the first twenty years of my life in Austria. After all, it was the language of my mother's care, my father's rule, the language of my formal schooling—and so it had become mine. Or I had become it.

I assumed that I could translate with Sade and with our dictionary apps and add cultural and contextual knowledge. I assumed I was an expert on deeper meaning and application of German words.

I wasn't.

Sade's work, *Härte*, isn't about source and target texts or about linear accuracy and conventional fidelity. *Härte* is circular and wavelike, steel-soft, ungraspable, and precisely cutting.

It is an invention of a new language, a remaking of our stale language, and an intervention into the inherent violence of our words. It is a multilingual questionnaire, an accusation, and an embrace. It is, to me, the anti-gaslight.

Being a dictionary while exploring *Härte* opened my language to me on a more essential and primal level. Sade's instruction was never, "translate this." It was, "what German words you know does this phrase sound like?" What German words in the emotional realm of *Härte* does this sound like? I couldn't draw on my usual inventory of bilingual vocabulary. I had to let the sounds and connotations of *Härte*'s phrases sink into me, had to let them reverberate down into and through my intestines. For the first time, I felt the fierce emotional resonances of syllables. I began to search through the musical mud for expressions that could carry what I knew about sexual objectification and trauma. As a word-book (or better: word-body) I would then suggest German words or, more often, give input on the wider context of Sade's already proposed transformations. Sade always considered all options, listened closely to the words hovering and echoing around and within us as we sat side by side on the wooden bench in a basement café until they knew a match had been found. This is how, for example, they transformed "rescue" into "Restkuh," which (in context) perfectly lays bare the subtext and the ominous, foreboding and constantly present violence of our unexamined hierarchies.

This process of finding language by undoing language with (another) language acted as a healing balm. While looking for, listening to, and finding words with Sade, I experienced a catharsis that I know *Härte* offers to every bruised human being who engages with it.

I am thankful to have been able to sit next to Sade during the initial phases of this book.

With gratitude/Willig gratis Duden
Maria G. Baker

Härte

Are you ready?
Are you rötlich?
Bist du Rettich?

Are you sure?
Are you Schur?
Bist du geschurt?

Did you like it?
Did you Leiche it?
Warst du Leiche?

Are you sure you didn't enjoy it?
Are you sure you didn't Engebeute it?
Steht fest du warst nicht enge Beute?

Are you a tease?
Are you a dies?
Bist du Diese?

Was it really rape?
Was it really Rappe?
Hat es wirklich gerappelt?

You invited him in didn't you?
You in weit him in didn't you?
Du warst ihm Weite, ja?

Are you irresponsible?
Are you ihre sponsern?
Bist du irre, Sponsor?

Can't you do anything right?
Can't you do anything Reit?
Kannst du ein Ding reiten?

Do you know anything?
Do you know innig Ding?
Bist du ein inniges Ding?

Have you ever stolen anything?
Have you ever Stollen anything?
Warst du jemals in einem Stollen?

Are you a liar?
Are you a Leier?
Bist du eine Leier?

Do you enjoy pain?
Do you enjoy Pein?
Magst du scheue Pein?

Are you leaving the house like that?
Are you Liebling the house?
Magst du mein Leiblingshaus?

What do you weigh these days?
What, do you weigh der Daak?
Bist du der Docht in eine finster Bude?

Are you still hungry?
Are you a stilled Hangrutsch?
Bist du ein Slidingslope?

Don't you worry about how people see you?
Don't you worry about people am See?
Ist die See allerhand Mutter?

Do you think you're innocent in all this?
Do you think you Reinmöse in all this?
Denkst du mit reiner Möse?

Don't you think it's time you grew up?
Don't you think it's time you Gruppe?
Denkst du Hochzeit ist eine Grube?

Are you too sensitive?

Are you Tugendsdieb?

Hat dich der Tugendsdieb besucht?

Don't you think you're overreacting?
Don't you think you're Ovarial-arterie?
Denkst du mit der Ovarialarterie?

Can you stop being so melodramatic?
Can you stop being Sommer lodert?
Kannst du den lodernden Sommer stoppen?

Can you stop being so needy?
Can you stop being so niedrig?
Kannst du aus der Niedrigkeit klettern?

Do you want to be poor forever?
Do you want to be Porree forever?
Willst du für immer Leaken?

Is that desperation I sense?
Is that desperation's Sense?
Erkennst du die späte Sense an?

Are you good at faking it?
Are you good at flecken it?
Bist du ein falscher Fleck?

Do you think you've earned that?
Do you think you Ferne that?
Sind deine Gedanken in der Ferne?

Is someone coming to rescue you?
Is someone coming to Restkuh?
Rettet keiner dich, du Restkuh du?

Do you pity your self?
Do you Pietät your selbst?
Bist du deine Pietät?

Will you ever be the person you want to be?
Will you ever biedere Person you want to be?
Kannst du beide Personen sein?

Can you protect yourself?
Can you Prostsekte yourself?
Bist du aus Brot und Sekt gemacht?

Isn't it incredible how articulate you're able to be?
Isn't it incredible Hauenartikulieren you're able to be?
Ist dein Artikulieren verhaut und unglaublich?

Can you make it on your own?
Can you Macke it on your own?
Kannst du Macken alleine machen?

Will you be alone forever?
Will you be ein Lohn forever?
Willst du nie deine Löhne heimzahlen?

Can you be in a relationship?
Can you be in a Relationsschiff?
Kannst du in das Rillenschiff steigen?

Are you afraid of your own shadow?
Are you erfreut of your own Schaden?
Wirfst du einen furchtsamen Schatten?

Is anyone allowed to touch you?
Is any one Anlaut to touch you?
Warum vertuschst du deine Laute?

Are you going to hold on to that forever?
Are you going to holt ein to that forever?
Holt deine Vergangenheit dich ein?

Can't you get over it already?
Can't you get Opfer it already?
Kannst du ein wehrloses Opfer sein?

Are you selfish?
Are you selbst Fisch?
Hast du eine Selbigkeit?

Are you cruel?
Are you Grölen?
Hörst du Grölen?

Are you even real?
Are you kiffen real?
Kiffst du zu viel?

Are you functioning?
Are you Funkhonig?
Isst du strahlend Honig?

Are you sick?
Are you Sieg?
Bist du ein sickernder Sieg?

Are you pointless?
Are you meutelos?
Wer lässt die Meute los?

Who do you desire?
Who do you die Seiher?
Ziehst du Auskunft ein deinem diesig Seiher Hirn?

Who are your people?
Who are Jahrbucher?
Wurst du mein Jahrbuch unterschreiben?

Would everyone be better off without you?
Would everyone be better ausgezogen?
Fühlst du dich wie ausgezogen?

Are you more trouble than you're worth?
Are you more Trubel als Wort?
Haben dich deine Worte heimgesucht?

Are you going to cry about it?
Are you going to Kreide about it?
Wieviel Kreide hast du gefressen?

Do they just tolerate you?
Do they just tolle Rate you?
Haben sie dich für einen tollen Preis gehalten?

Is your writing frivolous?
Is your Reihe frivol sein?
Wirst du wohl immer rein sein?

Are you a quitter?
Are you a Quitte?
Bist du ein Kitzwidder in Kotzwetter?

Are you powerful?
Are you Bauernsuhle?
Fühlst du dich den Mauerbauertraurigkeit?

How's your throat game?
What's your dröge Gäa like?
Schmuggelst du Drogen oder Gamba?

Who is preying on you?
Who is predigen for you?
Wie willst du sie prägen?

Is life worth living?
Do you want to, lieb?
Stimmst du dem Lüften zu?

Do you believe the worst part is over?
Do you believe the Wurstparte is over?
Blickst du die Wurst oft offen oder im Ofen an?

Tell the truth: does it hurt?
Tell the Trute: does it Herz?
Trübe trubelige Trute: ruft es Herzschmerz hervor?

Acknowledgments

A PREVIOUS DRAFT OF THIS POEM WAS PUBLISHED at the *Journal Petra* in 2016. An excerpt of *Härte* was published by Halophyte in 2018. A previous draft of this poem was published as part of Sade LaNay's MFA Thesis in Writing at the Pratt Institute in 2017.

My gratitude to the members of my cohort: Sasha Banks, Adriana Green, Lyric Hunter, Diamond Sharp, Laura Perez-Munoz, Ana Reyes-Bonar, Jive Poetic, Stevie Ruiz, Geoff Olsen, and Maria Baker; to the members of my thesis committee: Youmna Chlala, Sharifa Rhodes-Pitts, and Christian Hawkey; the Writing Studio faculty, The Marble House Project and the city of New York, specifically Brooklyn, specifically Bed-Stuy.